Manifest

Abundance

An interactive workbook

By

Lil Jon

&

Kabir Sehgal

Dedicated to you.

Keep persevering.

It will happen.

Published in 2024 by Tiger Turn

© 2024 Jonathan Smith and Kabir Sehgal

Printed in the United States of America.

ISBN: 9798300932787

First Edition

Manifesting Abundance Workbook

Manifesting is the process of turning your dreams into reality.

Table of Contents

Introduction

Heyyy.

Lil Jon here.

Let me guess what you're probably thinking. You're wondering what I'm doing here. You likely know me as a producer, DJ, rapper, television personality, or the King of Crunk. Yep, I am all these things.

But I also have another side.

I turned 50 a few years ago. I wasn't feeling quite right. Yeah, you could attribute some of my "ehh" feeling to natural aging. But I didn't like where I was in life. My physical and mental health both needed a reset. I did what most middle-aged men do: I got colonoscopy and thankfully everything turned out all right.

My doctor advised me to minimize and even stop drinking -- and to get healthy. So that's what I did. I started going to the gym, walking more, and just getting my physical self in shape. It made me feel so much better.

I also started meditating. At first, I didn't get it. Just sit in one place and take deep breaths? It was kind of boring. But I stuck with it, and I started to realize that boring is kind of the point. We all live frenetic lives that are full of constant noise and distractions. Meditation is the port in the storm, the safe place where you can go to relax and recharge.

Meditation became my habit. It has transformed me, my disposition, and just how I look at life. And naturally, I wanted to share my discovery with the world. If you find something good, you want to share it with a friend, right?

No, I'm not trying to be a New Age Guru or another celebrity advocating mindfulness. I'm simply trying to leverage my gifts and platform to share a positive message. You know me as an artist. So, I did what I normally do. I started making art.

I began making meditation music with Kabir Sehgal. We've released a few of albums with plans to make many more. The audience response has been bananas. Folks were surprised to hear me talking about meditation. Everyone thought of me as a fish-out-of-water. I'm known for having a wild and crazy party spirit. But now I'm saying that we should *turn down* to hear the voice within.

The overwhelming response made me think about how else I could help share this positive message. I know several folks who listen to my guided meditations every day. They tell me that these tracks have helped them get through difficult times or just feel better about life. I'm grateful to have played a small role in their journey.

I encourage you to listen to *Manifest Abundance*, our album of guided affirmations. Try repeating some of the affirmations that you hear like, "I am happy."

Trust me, I had my doubts at first. Just saying something isn't going to turn it into reality. But you'd be surprised how repeating an affirmation can really center your mind. You start to see the world through the prism of an affirmation. For example, when you say "I am happy" you might start noticing things that make you happier – like the sun or morning dew.

And then you feel a little bit happier.

About This Workbook

Manifesting your thoughts into action takes work. It takes commitment.

That's where this book comes in. I wanted to create this workbook so you could chronicle your progress. Yes, I want you to write your thoughts down in this book. Make this book yours. Carry it around with you. Make notes.

Chapters 2 through 9 are the affirmations that you can hear on *Manifest Abundance*. Chapters 10 through 21 are affirmations that we created especially for this workbook. Every chapter has a small worksheet that asks you a few questions. Please take the time to write down your responses. The sheer act of reflecting and writing will help get your mind moving in the right direction.

Chapter 22, the final chapter, includes 30 personal manifestation exercises. Treat this section as a daily journal. I'd like you to write your reflections every day for 30 days. It takes time to build a habit. But once you do, you can rely on automaticity. If you stick with this exercise, the day will come when your personal affirmations are like second nature. You'll wake up, say your affirmations, and you'll move throughout the day and gradually manifest your dreams.

I'm not here for myself. I'm here for you. I want you to live the life you've imagined. I believe you can accomplish anything that you put your mind to.

So, let's get going on this journey together.

Let's begin the work of attaining your dreams.

Chapter 2

Manifest Happiness

"For every minute you are angry you lose sixty seconds of happiness."
–Ralph Waldo Emerson

Happiness is something we crave and all deserve. I constantly think about my own happiness and how I can incorporate more of it into my life. By repeating these manifestations daily, I have noticed happiness amped up in my day-to-day life.

I am happy.

I am in good spirits.

I am joyful.

I am smiling.

I choose to be happy.

I choose happiness over sadness.

I choose joy over anger.

I welcome positive thoughts.

I deserve happiness every single day.

I am grateful for each moment of peace.

I am surrounded by light and joy.

I choose to be happy.

I choose happiness over sadness.

My happiness is a choice.

I choose joy over anger because it makes me feel good.

I welcome positive thoughts.

I learn from the negative and turn it into a positive.

I am relaxed.

I am taking it easy.

I am calm.

Everything is going just fine.

I am walking the path to greatness.

I feel clear, focused and centered.

I exude happiness to the world.

The universe is giving me happiness.

I release anything that is no longer serving me.

I am patient on my journey to happiness.

I am at peace.

I am grateful for each moment of peace.

I find joy in the simple things in life.

I am surrounded by positive happy people.

My happiness is my superpower.

Manifest happiness.

Manifestation Happiness Worksheet

1. How do you visualize your happiness?

_____

_____

_____

_____

_____

2. What do you think it will feel like to achieve your visualization?

_____

_____

_____

_____

_____

3. What will you do to achieve your visualization?

_____

_____

_____

_____

_____

4. How will you stay committed?

_____

_____

_____

_____

_____

5. How can you help others manifest happiness for themselves?

_____

_____

_____

_____

_____

Notes:

_____

_____

_____

_____

_____

_____

_____

_____

_____

_____

Chapter 3

Manifest Positivity

"Stand up to an obstacle. Just stand up to it, that's all, and don't give way under it, and it will finally break. You will break it. Something has to break, and it won't be you, it will be the obstacle."
–Norman Vincent Peale

Positivity, positivity, positivity. I say it ten times a day. Maintaining a positive mindset will change your life forever. Let go of negativity to make room for positivity—it's your new best friend. Once I started thinking more positively, everything in my world became brighter and clearer. Repeat these affirmations to yourself daily.

I radiate positivity.

I attract positivity.

I prioritize my mental and emotional well-being.

I choose to see the beauty and goodness in every situation.

I repeat these positive affirmations that nourish my mind.

I let go of comparison and celebrate my own unique journey.

I effortlessly attract positive and like-minded people into my life.

I am a magnet for positive opportunities and experiences.

I embrace each day with a positive mindset, an open heart.

I attract positivity into my life by focusing on what brings me joy.

I choose positive thoughts.

I attract positive relationships that uplift and inspire me.

I am deserving of all the positivity and happiness life has to offer.

I choose to let go of negativity.

I embrace positivity as my natural state of being.

I surround myself with relationships that support my mental health.

I set boundaries that protect my mental health and prioritize self-care.

I spread positivity to others.

I release fear and doubt.

I choose to focus on the positive aspects of others.

I choose to focus on the positive aspects of my life.

I am a beacon of positivity.

I thrive in an environment filled with positivity and love.

I have a good attitude.

I have a positive spirit.

I have a positive outlook on life.

Manifest positivity.

Manifestation Positivity Worksheet

1. How do you consciously bring positivity into your daily life?

_____
_____
_____
_____
_____

2. What changes in your mindset will help you embrace more positive thoughts?

_____
_____
_____
_____
_____

3. How do you handle negative situations while maintaining a positive outlook?

_____
_____
_____
_____
_____

4. How can you inspire and spread positivity to those around you?

_____

_____

_____

_____

Notes:

_____

_____

_____

_____

_____

_____

_____

_____

_____

_____

Chapter 4

Manifest Health

"We are healthy only to the extent that our ideas are humane."
--Kurt Vonnegut

My health improvements are what brought our albums and this book to fruition. Health rules our lives, and sometimes it's difficult to fully take control of it.

I am healthy.

I have good health.

I choose to have good health.

I am strong.

I am aware that my own thoughts can improve my health.

Every day I wake up, I am grateful.

I am flexible, agile, and quick.

I can move with ease.

I can heal and thrive.

My body is a miracle.

My body is strong and flexible.

I eat healthfully.

My body has all the nutrients it needs to keep me healthy.

My immune system is strong.

My blood pressure is stable.

My heart is strong.

I nourish my body.

My skin is smooth and clear.

I am filled with vitality and wellness.

I nourish my mind and my body.

My inner glow radiates.

I am resilient and filled with energy.

My teeth are straight and white.

My body is balanced in every way.

I am balanced physically.

I am balanced emotionally.

I am balanced mentally.

I nourish every cell of my body with my positive thinking.

My mind is powerful and makes my body do amazing things.

My mind is sharp.

My mind is restful.

I take care of myself.

Manifest health.

Manifest Health Worksheet

1. How do you envision your ideal state of health, both physically and mentally? Imagine and explain what this would look and feel like to you.

_____

_____

_____

_____

_____

2. What habits or routines will help you maintain your health goals?

_____

_____

_____

_____

_____

3. How will you stay motivated to prioritize your health every day?

_____

_____

_____

_____

_____

4. How can you encourage others to prioritize and manifest their own health?

_____

_____

_____

_____

_____

Notes:

_____

_____

_____

_____

_____

_____

_____

_____

_____

Radiate Your Light

Bring this image to life by adding vibrant colors that reflect the light within you.
Let your creativity shine as bright as your inner spirit.

Chapter 5

Manifest Opportunity

"Not knowing when the dawn will come I open every door."
--Emily Dickinson

If you want something, it helps to visualize it. No, you may not get what you want right away, but you would be surprised how the universe starts to respond to your desires...when you move with intention.

Opportunity presents themselves to us every day. If you don't think so, consider all the decisions you make within a day. These intentions gradually start to materialize. Every decision you make is an opportunity. If we don't take the time to recognize the opportunities we are given, we can never seize them.

The opportunities I receive make me grow as a person.

Opportunity is not just about money or material goods.

Opportunity can simply make me, and others feel good.

Opportunity can make me grow as a person.

Opportunity is not always about what I get.

I have an opportunity to serve others.

I have an opportunity to help others succeed.

I have opportunities come from anywhere, at any time.

Opportunities will find me.

I am so grateful for the opportunities I have been given.

I am open to receive new opportunities.

I am excited to see what comes next.

I am a magnet for opportunity.

I say yes to opportunities.

I am confident in seizing the right opportunities for me.

I attract opportunities by the thoughts that I think.

I attract opportunities by the words I speak.

I attract opportunities by the actions I take.

I am thoughtful about which opportunities I pursue.

Every day brings fresh opportunities my way.

Opportunities flow into my life.

I put myself in the right place and the right time for new opportunities.

I am grateful for the opportunities that come my way.

I embrace the opportunities for growth.

I accept transformation.

Manifest opportunity.

Manifest Opportunity Worksheet

1. How do you recognize and create opportunities in your life?

_____

_____

_____

_____

_____

2. What actions will you take to attract more opportunities aligned with your goals?

_____

_____

_____

_____

_____

3. How will you overcome fear or hesitation when new opportunities arise?

_____

_____

_____

_____

_____

4. How can you help others recognize and seize opportunities in their own lives?

_____

_____

_____

_____

_____

Notes:

_____

_____

_____

_____

_____

_____

_____

_____

_____

Chapter 6

Manifest Love

"There is nothing I would not do for those who are really my friends. I have no
notion of loving people by halves, it is not my nature."
--Jane Austin

Love is what makes the world go round—a phenomenon so epic that we can't quite
put our finger on it. The love between friends, family, and personal relationships is
truly powerful. Let's open our hearts.

If you want to be loved, you must first love yourself.

I love myself.

I am open to love.

I am open to the world.

I accept love into my life.

I am deserving of love.

I am open to receiving love from others.

I am ready to be loved.

I am loved.

I give love in return.

I love that I can give and receiving love.

All things are possible.

The universe wants me to be happy.

I love my life.

I love my family.

I love my friends.

I love those who love me.

Love is all there is.

I love who I am.

I am loved for all the good that I do for others.

I attract loving and supportive relationships.

My heart is filled with love and compassion for all beings.

Love is the foundation of all my actions and decisions.

I am open to experiencing love in all its beautiful forms.

The love I give comes back to me, multiplied.

Love is abundant in my life.

I am capable of loving others.

I set clear boundaries for the love I want to receive.

I am deeply loved by the universe.

I embody love and kindness in all my interactions.

I am grateful for the love I receive.

Love flows through me.

I have harmony in my relationships.

Manifest love.

Manifest Love Worksheet

1. How do you visualize love showing up in your life, both from yourself and others?

_____

_____

_____

_____

_____

2. What actions will you take to cultivate and nurture self-love?

_____

_____

_____

_____

_____

3. How can you open yourself up to receiving love from others?

_____

_____

_____

_____

_____

4. How will you share and express love to those around you?

_____

_____

_____

_____

_____

Notes:

_____

_____

_____

_____

_____

_____

_____

_____

_____

Chapter 7

Manifest Acceptance

"Life is a series of natural and spontaneous changes. Don't resist them. That only creates sorrow. Let reality be reality. Let things flow naturally forward in whatever way they like."
--Lao Tzu

Acceptance is a steppingstone in our lives that we must face to process and move forward freely. Manifesting acceptance is so incredibly powerful because it can spark transformative positive changes in your life that you may have been ignoring.

I accept who I am.

I am open to receiving what the universe is telling me.

I accept that everything is meant to be.

I accept that everything has its place in the world.

I accept that things don't need to make sense for them to exist.

I accept if someone thinks differently from me.

I understand that all things are pure energy.

I live in the present moment.

I accept that I am not in control of what happens around me.

I accept that I am in control of how I react.

I accept my responsibilities with pleasure.

I accept those in my life.

I am at peace with myself and my place in the world.

If an apology does come, I accept and forgive.

I forgive to give

I accept my relationship with myself and others.

I accept things that are difficult.

Today I accept.

I accept to give myself peace.

Everything is all right.

Everything is all right.

I embrace my uniqueness.

I release my need for control and find peace in acceptance.

I am surrounded by love and acceptance.

I accept my past as a part of my growth.

I am in touch with my inner peace.

I honor my feelings.

I trust the process of life.

Manifest acceptance.

Manifest Acceptance Worksheet

1. What areas of your life require more acceptance and understanding?

_____

_____

_____

_____

_____

2. How can you practice self-acceptance, even when things don't go as planned?

_____

_____

_____

_____

_____

3. How can accepting situations outside of your control bring you peace?

_____

_____

_____

_____

_____

4. How can you show acceptance and compassion toward others, even when their views or actions differ from your own?

_____

_____

_____

_____

_____

Notes:

_____

_____

_____

_____

_____

_____

_____

_____

_____

Chapter 8

Manifest Abundancy

"Life becomes fulfilling only when you act from the level of meaning."
--Deepak Chopra

Abundance... oh yeah. Let's manifest all the things in our lives that we wish were more abundance. Let's not forget all the abundance we already have. Abundance flows through all our lives.

It's better to give than to receive.

I give abundantly.

I think abundantly.

I imagine abundantly.

I live abundantly.

I receive abundantly.

I love abundantly.

I am a magnet to positive experiences.

What I think, I attract.

I surround myself with abundance and substance.

I love to give everything I must give.

I am abundant in my health.

Abundancy exists in every area of my life.

Abundance flows into my life.

I am grateful for all the abundancy I have now.

My mind is abundant with positivity.

I am satisfied due to my abundancy.

Abundance is my natural state.

I am open to receiving all the good life has to offer.

I celebrate the abundance around me.

My life is filled of joyful and rich experiences.

Manifest abundance.

Manifest Abundance Worksheet

1. Visualize abundance in your life—financially, emotionally, and spiritually. Write down -- word for word -- what you see.

_____

_____

_____

_____

_____

2. What steps will you take to open yourself up to receiving more abundance?

_____

_____

_____

_____

_____

3. How can practicing gratitude enhance the abundance you attract?

_____

_____

_____

_____

_____

4. How can you share the abundance you receive with others to create a positive cycle?

_____

_____

_____

_____

_____

Notes:

_____

_____

_____

_____

_____

_____

_____

_____

_____

_____

_____

Calm and Collected

Immerse yourself in this moment of calm and peace, adding your personal touch to reflect serenity. What colors will you choose?

Chapter 9

Manifest Anything

"Everything you can imagine is real."
--Pablo Picasso

If you want something, you first must imagine it. It can be difficult to ask yourself what you really want out of life. It should be something that makes you happy.

I manifest anything I want by first imagining it.

I am not limited by anything other than my own imagination.

It feels good to imagine my success.

I can manifest anything.

My manifestations will translate into reality.

I am worthy of my success.

I attract positive opportunities.

I manifest everything desire.

I am surrounded by abundance and prosperity.

I trust myself and my intuition.

I am confident in my abilities.

I deserve all the good things that come my way.

I welcome new possibilities.

I am filled with positive energy.

I manifest my ideal life every single day.

I will receive everything I want.

I am aligned with what I want and what I need.

I am always learning.

I am in control of my thoughts and emotions.

I am open to receiving miracles and blessings.

I am constantly evolving into the best version of myself.

I am proud of my achievements.

I am grateful for the present moment.

I live the life that I imagine.

My imagination is a powerful tool.

I trust that I will receive everything I need at the perfect time.

I align my goals everyday with my aspirations.

I take inspired actions that lead me to my goals.

Manifest anything.

Manifest Anything Worksheet

1. What is the one thing you truly want to manifest in your life right now. Why?

_____
_____
_____
_____
_____

2. How do you visualize yourself living in alignment with this desire or goal?

_____
_____
_____
_____
_____

3. What actions or steps will you take to bring your manifestation into reality?

_____
_____
_____
_____
_____

4. How can you overcome self-doubt and stay focused on manifesting what you want?

_____

_____

_____

_____

_____

Notes:

_____

_____

_____

_____

_____

_____

_____

_____

_____

_____

Chapter 10

Manifest Dreams

"All our dreams can come true, if we have the courage to pursue them."
–Walt Disney

Dream big like I do. I promise you can achieve anything you set your mind to.

I am worthy of my dreams.

I dream big.

I believe in my ability to achieve those dreams.

My dreams are my guide, leading me toward my highest potential.

I trust the universe to help me manifest my dreams into reality.

I am taking the steps needed to turn my dreams into actions.

I am open to receiving guidance and inspiration from the world around me.
I believe my dreams.

I believe in my vision.

Every challenge I face is an opportunity to get closer to my dreams.

Every day, I move closer to living my dream life.

I have the power to manifest my dreams through my thoughts, actions, and persistence.

I allow myself to dream without limits.

I follow my dreams with courage.

My dreams are within my reach.

I deserve to live the life I dream.

I trust the process of life.

I am patient as my dreams unfold.

I attract the people, opportunities, and resources that align with my dreams.

I am grateful for the opportunities that bring my dreams to life.

I persevere in the pursuit of my dreams.

I am always evolving, and my dreams expand as I grow.

Every step towards my dreams is valuable.

My passion fuels my dreams.

I visualize my dreams clearly.

I surround myself with support that encourages my dreams.

Manifest dreams.

Manifest Dreams Worksheet

1. What is your biggest dream, and how do you envision it becoming a reality?

_____

_____

_____

_____

_____

2. What emotions will you feel when you achieve your dream, and how do those emotions motivate you?

_____

_____

_____

_____

_____

3. What specific steps will you take to move closer to making your dream come true?

_____

_____

_____

_____

_____

4. How can you stay resilient and focused when challenges arise on the path to achieving your dream?

_____

_____

_____

_____

_____

Notes:

_____

_____

_____

_____

_____

_____

_____

_____

_____

Chapter 11

Manifest Confidence

"You gain strength, courage and confidence by every experience in which you really stop to look fear in the face."
--Eleanor Roosevelt

A lack of confidence will hold you back from realizing your full potential. Have confidence in achieving your goals. Confidence is a tool that can elevate every area of your life. Let's manifest the confidence that you need.

I am confident in who I am.

I trust in my abilities and strengths.

I do not compare myself to others.

I am confident in my decisions.

I am enough.

Everything I want also wants me.

I believe in myself and know that I can overcome any challenge.

My confidence grows with every step I take toward my goals.

I embrace my uniqueness and show up as my authentic self.

I radiate confidence in everything I do.

I speak clearly and assertively, knowing my voice matters.

I am worthy of success and capable of achieving my dreams.

I am resilient, and I bounce back stronger from every setback.

I am comfortable in my own skin and embrace my individuality.

I move forward with confidence.

Every day, my confidence grows as I act toward my goals.

I believe in my vision.

I pursue it with determination and grace.

I let go of self-doubt and welcome self-assurance.

I trust in the process of learning and growing, knowing that confidence comes with experience.

I know that challenges are temporary.

I have the inner strength to overcome them.

I am proud of who I am and how far I've come.

I am fearless in the pursuit of my dreams and goals.

I inspire others with my confidence, courage, and optimism.

I believe in my ability to create the life I desire.

I am constantly evolving, becoming the best version of myself with every new experience.

I am open to growth and learning, knowing that with each step, my confidence expands.

I trust the universe to support me as I manifest confidence in all that I do.

Manifest confidence.

Manifest Confidence Worksheet

1. What areas of your life would benefit the most from increased confidence?

_____

_____

_____

_____

_____

2. How do you visualize yourself acting and feeling when you are fully confident?

_____

_____

_____

_____

_____

3. What daily actions can you take to build and reinforce your confidence?

_____

_____

_____

_____

_____

4. How can you maintain your confidence when faced with doubt or criticism?

_____

_____

_____

_____

_____

Notes:

_____

_____

_____

_____

_____

_____

_____

_____

_____

_____

Chapter 12

Manifest Respect

"I speak to everyone in the same way, whether he is the garbage man or the president of the university."
--Albert Einstein

Manifesting respect will build a stronger foundation for all your relationships, including the one with yourself. Respect starts within.

I respect myself and my journey.

I am worthy of the respect of others.

I give respect in return.

I honor my values and live in alignment with them.

I treat others with kindness.

I receive the same in return.

Others respect my boundaries.

I respect the boundaries of others.

I am proud of who I am.

I carry myself with dignity.

I communicate openly and respectfully in all my relationships.

I am deserving of respect for my efforts, my talents, and my contributions.

I respect my time, energy, and resources, knowing they are valuable.

I attract people who value and respect me for who I am.

I respect the uniqueness of others and celebrate diversity.

I choose to focus on mutual respect and understanding in my interactions.

I honor my worth and stand up for what I believe in with confidence.

I trust that I am respected by those around me because I respect myself.

I value my personal growth and honor my achievements, big and small.

I show respect through my actions.

I understand that respect begins with self-love and self-acceptance.

I deserve to be treated with respect in all areas of my life.

I respect the process of learning and growing.

I welcome relationships filled with mutual respect, kindness, and compassion.

I radiate respect, and it returns to me in all forms.

Manifest respect.

Manifest Respect Worksheet

1. How do you define respect, both for yourself and for others?

_____
_____
_____
_____
_____

2. In what ways can you show yourself more respect in your daily life?

_____
_____
_____
_____
_____

3. How can you earn and maintain the respect of those around you?

_____
_____
_____
_____
_____

4. How will you demonstrate respect to others, even in challenging situations?

_____

_____

_____

_____

_____

Notes:

_____

_____

_____

_____

_____

_____

_____

_____

Chapter 13

Manifest Kindness

"Be kind, for everyone you meet is fighting a harder battle."
–Plato

Kindness is the practice of generosity and thoughtfulness. It means offering acts of service freely, without expectation or ulterior motives. True kindness comes from the heart, lifting spirits, reducing loneliness, and fostering a sense of purpose. It's a gift that's never wasted. We should strive to nurture and share the kindness within us every day.

I am kind to myself and others.

I choose to lead with kindness in all situations.

Kindness flows naturally from me and touches everyone I meet.

I believe in the power of small acts of kindness to make a big impact.

I treat others with compassion.

I am patient with their journey.

I attract kind and loving energy into my life.

I speak kind words and think kind thoughts.

I am surrounded by kindness.

I give kindness freely.

I know that kindness brings peace to my heart and mind.

I lead by example, spreading kindness through my actions.

I am grateful for the kindness that others show me.

I return kindness tenfold.

I choose to be gentle and understanding.

I create a world filled with kindness.

I forgive easily and let go of any negative emotions that block kindness.

I treat myself with the same kindness and compassion that I show to others.

I believe that kindness can heal wounds, uplift spirits, and inspire change.

I seek opportunities to share kindness in every aspect of my life.

I am a magnet for kind-hearted people and positive experiences.

I trust in the power of kindness to create a ripple effect of goodness.

I know that being kind to myself is the foundation for being kind to others.

I choose kindness as my way of life, spreading joy and love wherever I go.

I am kind.

Manifest kindness.

Manifest Kindness Worksheet

1. How can you show more kindness to yourself daily?

_____

_____

_____

_____

_____

2. In what ways can you incorporate acts of kindness into your interactions with others?

_____

_____

_____

_____

_____

3. How do you feel when you both give and receive kindness, and how does that inspire you?

_____

_____

_____

_____

_____

4. What challenges do you face in practicing kindness, and how can you overcome them?

_____

_____

_____

_____

_____

Notes:

_____

_____

_____

_____

_____

_____

_____

_____

_____

Still the Mind

*A moment of stillness, inviting a thoughtful blend of colors
to reflect the quiet power of a still mind.*

Chapter 14

Manifest Determination

"I have discovered in life that there are ways of getting almost anywhere you want to go, if you really want to go."
–Langston Hughes

Determination isn't exclusive. It's within everyone, fueled by personal experiences and the desire for growth.

I am determined to achieve my goals.

I have the strength and resilience to overcome any obstacle.

Every step I take brings me closer to my dreams.

I trust in my ability to persevere, no matter the challenges.

I am focused and committed to my path.

I am determined.

I approach every task with determination and confidence.

I push forward even in the face of any adversity.

I believe in my capacity to achieve great things.

I am not afraid of setbacks.

I see them as opportunities to grow stronger.

I have the inner strength to keep going, even when the road is tough.

I am disciplined in my actions and consistent in my efforts.

I welcome challenges to prove my determination.

I am determined to succeed, and I never give up on what I believe in.

I embrace the journey, knowing that determination is the key to my success.

I turn my dreams into reality through determination.

I am relentless in pursuing my goals.

I trust in my ability to achieve them.

I am driven by my purpose, and nothing can deter me from my path.

I trust the process, knowing that my determination will lead me to victory.

I am a force of nature, unstoppable.

Nothing can get in my way in the pursuit of success.

I am laser focused.

I celebrate every milestone, knowing that each one is a testament to my determination.

I am determined to live the life I envision for myself.

Manifest determination.

Manifest Determination Worksheet

1. What is a specific goal you want to achieve, and how can determination help you reach it?

_____

_____

_____

_____

_____

2. How will you stay focused and determined when faced with obstacles or setbacks?

_____

_____

_____

_____

_____

3. What daily habits or practices can strengthen your determination?

_____

_____

_____

_____

_____

4. How can you inspire others around you to be more determined in pursuing their goals?

_____

_____

_____

_____

_____

Notes:

_____

_____

_____

_____

_____

_____

_____

_____

_____

Chapter 15

Manifest Courage

"Courage is the most important of all the virtues because without courage, you can't practice any other virtue consistently."
--Maya Angelou

Fear and doubt may cloud your mind, but they're only passing thoughts—not your truth. Let them drift away as you step boldly into courage.

I am courageous.

I stand tall.

I am brave and strong in the face of fear.

Courage flows through me with every step I take.

I trust in my ability to handle any challenges that come my way.

I embrace uncertainty with confidence and faith in myself.

I face my fears head-on and grow stronger each time I do.

I have the courage to pursue my dreams, no matter how big they seem.

I am bold in acting toward the life I desire.

I choose courage over comfort, knowing that growth lies beyond my comfort zone.

I am proud of my inner strength and resilience.

I speak my truth with courage, even when it feels difficult.

I have the power to stand up for myself and my beliefs.

I welcome change and face new experiences with an open heart and mind.

I trust that every step forward, no matter how small, is an act of courage.

I am unshakable in my pursuit of what matters most to me.

I have the courage to make bold decisions that align with my values.

I believe in my ability to overcome adversity with grace and bravery.

I am fearless in expressing my authentic self to the world.

I let go of fear and embrace the unknown with courage and trust.

I am courageous in both my thoughts and actions.

I inspire others with my bravery and determination.

I am strong, resilient, and full of courage in all that I do.

Fear is not in control. I am.

My courage is my strength.

I am fearless and limitless.

Manifest courage.

Manifest Courage Worksheet

1. What fears or challenges are you currently facing that require courage to overcome?

_____

_____

_____

_____

_____

2. How do you envision yourself acting with courage in situations where you usually feel hesitant?

_____

_____

_____

_____

_____

3. What daily actions can you take to build your courage and push beyond your comfort zone?

_____

_____

_____

_____

_____

4. How can showing courage inspire others around you to be brave in their own lives?

_____
_____
_____
_____
_____

Notes:

_____
_____
_____
_____
_____
_____
_____
_____
_____
_____

Chapter 16

Manifest Willpower

"What is now proved was once only imagined."
–William Blake

When I first began my wellness journey, my doctor advised me to quit drinking, partying, and other habits that had become deeply embedded in my life. It took immense willpower for me to break these habits. Learning to say "no" is a superpower that restores control over your life. Fortunately, you know someone who has walked this path—me.

I believe in my willpower.

I have willpower that guides me toward my goals.

I am disciplined and focused in all that I do.

I have the strength to resist distractions.

My willpower grows stronger each time I use it.

I am in control of my thoughts, actions, and decisions.

I have the power to make choices that align with my values and dreams.

I am determined, and my willpower drives me to succeed.

I follow through on my commitments with my persistence and focus.

I resist temptation.

I have the self-control to push through challenges.

I respect my willpower.

I am confident in my ability to overcome obstacles with my willpower.

I trust my inner strength to guide me in every situation.

I take control of my habits and create routines that support my success.

I am patient with myself, knowing that progress takes time and effort.

I have the power to delay immediate gratification in favor of long-term success.

I stay true to my path, even when it feels difficult or uncertain.

I will remain in charge of my destiny.

I use my willpower to shape my future.

I welcome challenges as opportunities to strengthen my resolve.

I am proud of my unwavering commitment to my goals.

I manifest my desires through consistent effort, driven by my willpower.

My willpower is strong and resilient.

Manifest willpower.

Manifest Willpower Workbook

1. What specific goals do you want to achieve that require willpower?

_____

_____

_____

_____

_____

2. How do you stay disciplined and maintain willpower when faced with temptation or distractions?

_____

_____

_____

_____

_____

3. What strategies can you implement to strengthen your willpower daily?

_____

_____

_____

_____

_____

4. How can you inspire and support others in developing their own willpower?

_____

_____

_____

_____

_____

Notes:

_____

_____

_____

_____

_____

_____

_____

_____

Chapter 17

Manifest Decisiveness

"If you do not change direction, you may end up where you are heading."
--Siddhārtha Gautama

Every day, our lives present us with both small and big decisions. By practicing decisiveness, you will strengthen your decision-making abilities. Choices that once felt challenging may become easier as you practice and embrace these empowering manifestations.

I am confident in my ability to make clear and effective decisions.

I trust myself to choose wisely and act swiftly.

I make decisions with ease, knowing that I am in control of my path.

I have the courage to make bold choices, even when faced with uncertainty.

I release the fear of making the wrong decision and trust the process.

I take decisive action.

I believe in my judgment and intuition.

I move forward with confidence, knowing that every decision I make leads to growth.

I make decisions that align with my values and long-term goals.

I trust that each choice I make brings me closer to success.

I embrace responsibility for my decisions and learn from every experience.

I act with clarity and purpose.

I am in control of my life.

I do not let indecision hold me back.

I understand I will not always be correct, and that is OK.

I am decisive in both small and big matters, shaping my life with intention.

I trust my instincts and confidently follow through on my decisions.

I know that every decision that I make contributes to my personal growth.

I can make powerful decisions that propel me toward my dreams.

I am decisive, strong, and clear in my choices.

Manifest decisiveness.

Manifest Decisiveness Worksheet

1. What areas of your life could benefit from more decisive action, and why?

_____

_____

_____

_____

_____

2. How do you feel when you make a confident and timely decision?

_____

_____

_____

_____

_____

3. What steps can you take to improve your decision-making process and trust yourself more?

_____

_____

_____

_____

_____

4. How can you help others around you become more decisive in their own lives?

_____

_____

_____

_____

_____

Notes:

_____

_____

_____

_____

_____

_____

_____

_____

Chapter 18

Manifest Power

"Ultimately, the only power to which man should aspire is that which he exercises
over himself."
–Elie Wiesel

Influence and control are sensitive forces to manifest. Let's take a moment to align ourselves before we begin. Our goal is to gain power over our own lives, not over the lives of others. Remember, your words are powerful. Use your influence respectfully and responsibly. By mastering your mind, you unlock the power to uplift and help others.

I am powerful.

I embrace my inner strength.

I stand tall in my power.

I trust in my ability to influence my own life and the world around me.

I am in control of my thoughts, actions, and destiny.

I have the power to overcome any obstacle.

I am confident in my ability to take charge and lead with purpose.

I harness my power to pursue my dreams and manifest my desires.

I step into every situation with strength and determination.

I believe I will achieve greatness through the power within me.

I use my power wisely and responsibly, for the good of myself and others.

I trust myself to make decisions that reflect my power and vision.

I am a force of nature.

I am resilient and powerful, no matter what life throws my way.

I tap into my inner power to take bold action toward my goals.

I attract opportunities that allow me to express my full power.

I am fearless, knowing that my power comes from within and cannot be taken away.

I am aligned with my purpose.

I channel my power to achieve my highest potential.

I am powerful in both mind and spirit.

I trust myself to wield that power confidently.

I manifest my power in everything I do.

I trust my power to guide me to success.

Power flows through me.

I am powerful in my career.

I harness my power to do good.

I am grateful for my power.

Manifest power.

Manifest Power Worksheet

1. How do you define personal power?

_____

_____

_____

_____

_____

2. What actions can you take to reclaim and strengthen your sense of power?

_____

_____

_____

_____

_____

3. How can you use your personal power to take control of your goals and aspirations?

_____

_____

_____

_____

_____

4. How can you use your power to positively influence your environment and the people around you?

_____

_____

_____

_____

_____

Notes:

_____

_____

_____

_____

_____

_____

_____

_____

_____

Chapter 19

Manifest Compassion

"No one has ever become poor by giving."
--Anne Frank

Compassion is a gift that not only uplifts others but also enriches our own hearts. When I think of compassion, I aim to give it generously—far more than I ever expect in return. By choosing kindness, we foster deeper connections and remind ourselves that we're all navigating this life together.

I am compassionate of others.

I am compassionate to myself.

I exude compassion every day.

I lead with compassion in my interactions.

I am kind, understanding, and patient with myself and others.

I open my heart to empathy and see the world through others' eyes.

I choose to act with love and compassion in difficult situations.

I offer compassion freely, without judgment or expectation.

I am compassionate toward myself, embracing my imperfections with love.

I create space for others to express their feelings and experiences.

I am a source of comfort and support for everyone.

I listen with an open heart and respond with kindness.

I approach life with compassion, seeing the humanity in everyone.

I forgive easily, knowing that compassion heals wounds.

I trust that compassion will guide me to make thoughtful choices.

I am compassionate even when it's hard.

I treat myself with the same compassion I offer to others.

I radiate compassion and inspire others to do the same.

I understand that everyone is on their own journey.

I show everyone grace.

I find strength in compassion.

I attract people who value and express compassion in their lives.

I spread compassion wherever I go, making the world a kinder place.

I set out to give compassion every day.

I am compassionate to every creature.

I feel compassion flow through me.

Manifest compassion.

Manifest Compassion Worksheet

1. How can you show more compassion to yourself, especially during challenging times?

_____

_____

_____

_____

_____

2. What specific actions can you take to demonstrate compassion toward others in your daily life?

_____

_____

_____

_____

_____

3. How do you feel when you practice compassion?

_____

_____

_____

_____

_____

4. How can you cultivate a compassionate mindset, even when faced with difficult people or situations?

_____

_____

_____

_____

_____

Notes:

_____

_____

_____

_____

_____

_____

_____

_____

_____

Stretch to the Sun

Capture and color the warmth and energy that you feel from above and within.

Chapter 20

Manifest Strength

"The weak can never forgive. Forgiveness is the attribute of the strong."
--Mahatma Gandhi

Strength is enduring, humble, and transformative—a force that propels us forward, empowering us to overcome obstacles and grow with every experience. It's a guiding light that has carried me through life's most challenging moments, helping me emerge on the other side even stronger, more resilient, and ready to thrive.

I am strong.

I am strong physically and mentally.

I possess the strength to face any challenge that comes my way.

I trust in my ability to overcome hurdles and grow through adversity.

I am resilient.

I rise stronger after every setback.

I embrace my inner strength, which carries me through difficult times.

I have the power to persevere, even when the path is uncertain.

I am confident in my ability to handle whatever life throws at me.

I draw my strength from within.

I am capable of enduring and thriving, no matter the circumstances.

I trust my body and mind to provide the strength I need in every situation.

I welcome challenges as opportunities to reveal and strengthen my inner power.

I am unshakable.

My strength guides me toward success and fulfillment.

I am grateful for the strength that I possess and the resilience that I build each day.

I have the power to transform my challenges into growth and wisdom.

I am strong enough to stand tall and gentle enough to show compassion to others.

I trust that my strength will always carry me through, no matter the odds.

I celebrate my strength.

I draw strength from my past experiences.

I know that my strength is limitless, fueled by my belief in myself and my abilities.

I am deeply connected to the source of my inner strength. It grows with every breath.

I manifest strength in all areas of my life—physically, emotionally, mentally, and spiritually.

I embrace every opportunity to build my strength, trusting in my ability to thrive.

Manifest strength.

Manifest Strength Worksheet

1. How do you define inner strength?

_____

_____

_____

_____

_____

2. What personal challenges have helped you grow stronger?

_____

_____

_____

_____

_____

3. What daily practices or habits can you adopt to build your physical, emotional, and mental strength?

_____

_____

_____

_____

_____

4. How can you inspire and support others in manifesting their own strength?

_____

_____

_____

_____

_____

Notes:

_____

_____

_____

_____

_____

_____

_____

_____

_____

Chapter 21

Manifest Achievement

"No man needs sympathy because he has to work, because he has a burden to carry.
Far and away the best prize that life offers is the chance to work hard at work worth
doing."
--Theodore Roosevelt

OKAY! Let's celebrate completing these meaningful manifestations. Each
accomplishment builds on the last, reminding us of our potential and encouraging us
to strive for more. Achievements bring confidence, growth, and a sense of
fulfillment.

I can achieve anything I set my mind to.

I trust in my abilities and the process of achieving my goals.

I am focused, determined, and committed to my success.

Every step I take brings me closer to my goals.

I believe in my power to create the life I desire.

I am proud of the progress I make, no matter how small.

I embrace challenges as opportunities to grow and achieve more.

I celebrate my accomplishments and use them as fuel for future success.

I stay motivated and persistent, knowing that I am on the right path.

I attract opportunities that help me reach my goals with ease.

I set clear, achievable goals and act every day toward achieving them.

I trust in my ability to overcome obstacles.

I am driven by my passion and purpose.

I welcome success into my life.

I am grateful for every opportunity that leads to my achievements.

I do whatever it takes to achieve my goals.

I am surrounded by supportive people who encourage and celebrate my achievements.

I recognize and honor every achievement, big and small, in my journey.

I manifest achievement in all areas of my life.

I know that each day brings me closer to realizing my dreams.

I am an achiever.

I manifest success through my dedication and hard work.

Manifest achievement.

Manifest Achievement Worksheet

1. What are the key achievements you aspire to manifest?

_____

_____

_____

_____

_____

2. What steps will you take to turn your dreams into tangible achievements?

_____

_____

_____

_____

_____

3. How will you stay motivated and focused on your path to achieving success?

_____

_____

_____

_____

_____

4. How can you celebrate your achievements while continuing to strive for personal growth?

_____

_____

_____

_____

_____

Notes:

_____

_____

_____

_____

_____

_____

_____

_____

_____

_____

_____

_____

Om Shanti

A peaceful moment ready to be infused with calming colors that reflect your inner harmony.

Chapter 22

Personal Manifestation Exercises

Date: _____

I will manifest:

_____

_____

_____

My morning affirmation:

_____

_____

_____

_____

_____

My afternoon affirmation:

_____

_____

_____

_____

_____

My evening affirmation:

_____

_____

_____

_____

_____

My notes:

_____

_____

_____

_____

_____

_____

_____

_____

_____

_____

_____

_____

_____

Date: _____

I will manifest:

_____

_____

_____

My morning affirmation:

_____

_____

_____

_____

_____

My afternoon affirmation:

_____

_____

_____

_____

_____

My evening affirmation:

_____

_____

_____

_____

_____

My notes:

_____

_____

_____

_____

_____

_____

_____

_____

_____

_____

_____

_____

_____

Date: _____

I will manifest:

_____
_____
_____

My morning affirmation:

_____
_____
_____
_____
_____

My afternoon affirmation:

_____
_____
_____
_____
_____

My evening affirmation:

_____

_____

_____

_____

_____

My notes:

_____

_____

_____

_____

_____

_____

_____

_____

_____

_____

_____

_____

_____

Date: _____

I will manifest:

_____

_____

_____

My morning affirmation:

_____

_____

_____

_____

_____

My afternoon affirmation:

_____

_____

_____

_____

_____

My evening affirmation:

_____
_____
_____
_____
_____

My notes:

_____
_____
_____
_____
_____
_____
_____
_____
_____
_____
_____
_____
_____

Date: _____

I will manifest:

_____
_____
_____

My morning affirmation:

_____
_____
_____
_____
_____

My afternoon affirmation:

_____
_____
_____
_____
_____

My evening affirmation:

_____

_____

_____

_____

_____

My notes:

_____

_____

_____

_____

_____

_____

_____

_____

_____

_____

_____

_____

Date: _____

I will manifest:

_____
_____
_____

My morning affirmation:

_____
_____
_____
_____
_____

My afternoon affirmation:

_____
_____
_____
_____
_____

My evening affirmation:

_____

_____

_____

_____

_____

My notes:

_____

_____

_____

_____

_____

_____

_____

_____

_____

_____

_____

_____

_____

Date: _____

I will manifest:

_____

_____

_____

My morning affirmation:

_____

_____

_____

_____

_____

My afternoon affirmation:

_____

_____

_____

_____

_____

My evening affirmation:

_____

_____

_____

_____

_____

My notes:

_____

_____

_____

_____

_____

_____

_____

_____

_____

_____

_____

_____

_____

Date: _____

I will manifest:

_____
_____
_____

My morning affirmation:

_____
_____
_____
_____
_____

My afternoon affirmation:

_____
_____
_____
_____
_____

My evening affirmation:

_____

_____

_____

_____

_____

My notes:

_____

_____

_____

_____

_____

_____

_____

_____

_____

_____

_____

_____

Date: _____

I will manifest:

_____

_____

_____

My morning affirmation:

_____

_____

_____

_____

_____

My afternoon affirmation:

_____

_____

_____

_____

_____

My evening affirmation:

_____
_____
_____
_____
_____

My notes:

_____
_____
_____
_____
_____
_____
_____
_____
_____
_____
_____
_____
_____
_____

Date: _____

I will manifest:

_____

_____

_____

My morning affirmation:

_____

_____

_____

_____

_____

My afternoon affirmation:

_____

_____

_____

_____

_____

My evening affirmation:

_____

_____

_____

_____

_____

My notes:

_____

_____

_____

_____

_____

_____

_____

_____

_____

_____

_____

_____

Date: _____

I will manifest:

_____

_____

_____

My morning affirmation:

_____

_____

_____

_____

_____

My afternoon affirmation:

_____

_____

_____

_____

_____

My evening affirmation:

_____

_____

_____

_____

_____

My notes:

_____

_____

_____

_____

_____

_____

_____

_____

_____

_____

_____

_____

_____

Date: _____

I will manifest:

_____

_____

_____

My morning affirmation:

_____

_____

_____

_____

_____

My afternoon affirmation:

_____

_____

_____

_____

_____

My evening affirmation:

_____

_____

_____

_____

_____

My notes:

_____

_____

_____

_____

_____

_____

_____

_____

_____

_____

_____

_____

_____

Date: _____

I will manifest:

_____

_____

_____

My morning affirmation:

_____

_____

_____

_____

_____

My afternoon affirmation:

_____

_____

_____

_____

_____

My evening affirmation:

_____

_____

_____

_____

_____

My notes:

_____

_____

_____

_____

_____

_____

_____

_____

_____

_____

_____

_____

_____

The Stars Above

Illuminate with colors that capture the endless wonder of the skies.

Date: _____

I will manifest:

_____

_____

_____

My morning affirmation:

_____

_____

_____

_____

_____

My afternoon affirmation:

_____

_____

_____

_____

_____

My evening affirmation:

_____

_____

_____

_____

_____

My notes:

_____

_____

_____

_____

_____

_____

_____

_____

_____

_____

_____

_____

_____

Date: _____

I will manifest:

_____
_____
_____

My morning affirmation:

_____
_____
_____
_____
_____

My afternoon affirmation:

_____
_____
_____
_____
_____

My evening affirmation:

_____

_____

_____

_____

_____

My notes:

_____

_____

_____

_____

_____

_____

_____

_____

_____

_____

_____

_____

Date: _____

I will manifest:

_____

_____

_____

My morning affirmation:

_____

_____

_____

_____

_____

My afternoon affirmation:

_____

_____

_____

_____

_____

My evening affirmation:

_____
_____
_____
_____
_____

My notes:

_____
_____
_____
_____
_____
_____
_____
_____
_____
_____
_____
_____
_____

Date: _____

I will manifest:

_____
_____
_____

My morning affirmation:

_____
_____
_____
_____
_____

My afternoon affirmation:

_____
_____
_____
_____
_____

My evening affirmation:

_____

_____

_____

_____

_____

My notes:

_____

_____

_____

_____

_____

_____

_____

_____

_____

_____

_____

_____

_____

Date: _____

I will manifest:

_____
_____
_____

My morning affirmation:

_____
_____
_____
_____
_____

My afternoon affirmation:

_____
_____
_____
_____
_____

My evening affirmation:

_____

_____

_____

_____

_____

My notes:

_____

_____

_____

_____

_____

_____

_____

_____

_____

_____

_____

_____

Date: _____

I will manifest:

_____
_____
_____

My morning affirmation:

_____
_____
_____
_____
_____

My afternoon affirmation:

_____
_____
_____
_____
_____

My evening affirmation:

_____

_____

_____

_____

_____

My notes:

_____

_____

_____

_____

_____

_____

_____

_____

_____

_____

_____

_____

_____

Date: _____

I will manifest:

_____
_____
_____

My morning affirmation:

_____
_____
_____
_____
_____

My afternoon affirmation:

_____
_____
_____
_____
_____

My evening affirmation:

_____

_____

_____

_____

_____

My notes:

_____

_____

_____

_____

_____

_____

_____

_____

_____

_____

_____

_____

Date: _____

I will manifest:

_____
_____
_____

My morning affirmation:

_____
_____
_____
_____
_____

My afternoon affirmation:

_____
_____
_____
_____
_____

My evening affirmation:

_____

_____

_____

_____

_____

My notes:

_____

_____

_____

_____

_____

_____

_____

_____

_____

_____

_____

_____

Confident Posture

*An expression of posture and confidence, waiting for your colors
to bring out its strength and grace.*

Date: _____

I will manifest:

_____
_____
_____ . _____

My morning affirmation:

_____
_____
_____
_____
_____

My afternoon affirmation:

_____
_____
_____
_____
_____

My evening affirmation:

_____
_____
_____
_____
_____

My notes:

_____
_____
_____
_____
_____
_____
_____
_____
_____
_____
_____
_____
_____

Date: _____

I will manifest:

_____

_____

_____

My morning affirmation:

_____

_____

_____

_____

_____

My afternoon affirmation:

_____

_____

_____

_____

_____

My evening affirmation:

_____

_____

_____

_____

_____

My notes:

_____

_____

_____

_____

_____

_____

_____

_____

_____

_____

_____

_____

_____

Date: _____

I will manifest:

_____

_____

_____

My morning affirmation:

_____

_____

_____

_____

_____

My afternoon affirmation:

_____

_____

_____

_____

_____

My evening affirmation:

_____

_____

_____

_____

_____

My notes:

_____

_____

_____

_____

_____

_____

_____

_____

_____

_____

_____

_____

_____

Date: _____

I will manifest:

_____
_____
_____

My morning affirmation:

_____
_____
_____
_____
_____

My afternoon affirmation:

_____
_____
_____
_____
_____

My evening affirmation:

_____

_____

_____

_____

_____

My notes:

_____

_____

_____

_____

_____

_____

_____

_____

_____

_____

_____

_____

Date: _____

I will manifest:

_____
_____
_____

My morning affirmation:

_____
_____
_____
_____
_____

My afternoon affirmation:

_____
_____
_____
_____
_____

My evening affirmation:

_____
_____
_____
_____
_____

My notes:

_____
_____
_____
_____
_____
_____
_____
_____
_____
_____
_____
_____
_____
_____

Date: _____

I will manifest:

_____
_____
_____

My morning affirmation:

_____
_____
_____
_____
_____

My afternoon affirmation:

_____
_____
_____
_____
_____

My evening affirmation:

_____

_____

_____

_____

_____

My notes:

_____

_____

_____

_____

_____

_____

_____

_____

_____

_____

_____

_____

Date: _____

I will manifest:

_____

_____

_____

My morning affirmation:

_____

_____

_____

_____

_____

My afternoon affirmation:

_____

_____

_____

_____

_____

My evening affirmation:

_____

_____

_____

_____

_____

My notes:

_____

_____

_____

_____

_____

_____

_____

_____

_____

_____

_____

_____

_____

Date: _____

I will manifest:

_____

_____

_____

My morning affirmation:

_____

_____

_____

_____

_____

My afternoon affirmation:

_____

_____

_____

_____

_____

My evening affirmation:

_____

_____

_____

_____

_____

My notes:

_____

_____

_____

_____

_____

_____

_____

_____

_____

_____

_____

_____

_____

About the Authors

Lil Jon

For over a decade, Lil Jon, the Grammy award-winning artist behind iconic catchphrases "YEAHHH," "OKAYY," and "WHATTT," has been a driving force in music and pop culture. Known for hits like "Turn Down For What" with DJ Snake and "Yeah!" with Usher and Ludacris, his influence spans from chart-topping tracks to viral moments. In 2024, he served as musical director for Usher's Super Bowl halftime show and launched his meditation albums, *Total Manifestation* and *Manifest Abundance*, to critical acclaim. Beyond music, Lil Jon's marketing savvy includes collaborations with brands like Pepsi, Peloton, and Don Julio, while his philanthropy includes building schools in Ghana with Pencils of Promise. As a global DJ, he's headlined residencies at top Las Vegas nightclubs and toured worldwide. With a career rooted in creating the Crunk movement and producing for stars like Britney Spears and Travis Barker, Lil Jon remains an enduring cultural icon.

Kabir Sehgal

Kabir Sehgal is a Multi-Grammy & Multi-Emmy winning producer, artist, composer, DJ. He's the Founder & CEO of Tiger Turn, a record label & production firm. He's the *New York Times* and *Wall Street Journal* bestselling author of 19 books including *Coined* and *Carry On*. He is a former vice president at J.P. Morgan & First Data. He is a US Navy Veteran who graduated from Dartmouth College and the London School of Economics.

Let's keep the conversation going. I share manifestations in *Wellness Wednesday* newsletter, I share quick affirmations, wellness tips, and soothing meditation music.

It's short and to the point.

Sign up at liljon.com